NATIONAL PARKS, MONUMENTS, AND HISTORIC SITES

Sticker, Color & Activity Book

chartwell books

Quarto

This edition published in 2025 by Chartwell Books,
an imprint of The Quarto Group
142 West 36th Street, 4th Floor
New York, NY 10018 USA
T (212) 779-4972
www.Quarto.com

Contains content originally published as *Harmonica* (2023), *Fabulous Food Boards* (2023), *National Parks Embroidery* (2024), and *Survive the Outdoors* (2024) by Chartwell Books, an imprint of The Quarto Group, 142 West 36th Street, 4th Floor, New York, NY 10018 USA.

10 9 8 7 6 5 4 3 2 1

Chartwell titles are also available at discount for retail, wholesale, promotional, and bulk purchase. For details, contact the Special Sales Manager by email at specialsales@quarto.com or by mail at The Quarto Group, Attn: Special Sales Manager, 100 Cummings Center Suite 265D, Beverly, MA 01915, USA.

ISBN: 978-0-7858-4628-4

Publisher: Wendy Friedman
Publishing Director: Meredith Mennitt
Editor: Jennifer Kushnier
Designer: Angelika Piwowarczyk
Image credits: Shutterstock

Mazes licensed from mazegenerator.net

Printed in Shaoguan, China. SL0525.

Celebrate the *diversity of the National Park Service!*

Established in 1916 by President Woodrow Wilson, the National Park Service (NPS) now oversees a network of more than 425 parks, preserves, recreation areas, and monuments across the United States. Covering more than 85 million acres, you'd have to cross the equator and venture north of the Arctic Circle to see them all!

In addition to the 63 places designated as official National Parks, there are hundreds of other places to visit. Each tells a chapter of our national story and helps conserve our natural and cultural heritage. From battlefields and military parks, to lakeshores and scenic trails, to historic sites and national parkways, they exist for the benefit of current and future generations.

Now you can get into the spirit of exploration and partake in some park-themed activities. Set your eyes on the 500+ detailed stickers featuring all manner of flora, fauna, nature scenes, and monuments; use them to decorate whatever you have at hand! There are also inspiring quotes from parks enthusiasts on the backs of the sticker pages for contemplation.

To add more fun to your free time, flip through the beautiful coloring pages, and test your brain with the variety of original puzzles, mazes, trivia, and matching games. Then try your hand at embroidery, geocaching, stargazing, and more with the instructions included in the book.

With so many activities to do and so much enjoyment to be had in these pages, *National Parks, Monuments, and Historic Sites Sticker, Color & Activity Book* is the perfect book when a free moment strikes. Whether you're a sticker lover, puzzler, history buff, or nature enthusiast, you're sure to find something unique in this cache of natural and historic beauty!

Park, Site & Monument Abbreviations

HP	Historical Park
IHS	International Historic Site
IP	International Park
NB	National Battlefield
NBP	National Battlefield Park
NCA	National Conservation Area
NF	National Forest
NHP & EP	National Historical Park & Ecological Preserve
NHL	National Historic Landmark
NH RES	National Historical Reserve
NHS	National Historic Site
NL	National Lakeshore
NM	National Monument
NM & PRES	National Monument & Preserve
NMP	National Military Park
N MEM	National Memorial
NNL	National Natural Landmark
NP	National Park
N & SP	National and State Parks
NP & PRES	National Park and Preserve
N PRES	National Preserve
NRA	National Recreation Area
NRRA	National River & Recreation Area
NSR	National Scenic River or Riverway
NST	National Scenic Trail
NWR	National Wildlife Refuge
PKWY	Parkway
WR	Wild River
WSR	Wild and Scenic River

Match the Track to the Animal!

With the vastness of the national park system—traversing desert, swamp, prairie, and snow-capped mountains—there's a variety of animal tracks to be found. See how many you can match.

Fox *Mink* *Duck* *Squirrel* *Goat*

Hare *Horse* *Eagle* *Raccoon* *Moose*

answers on the next page

Match the Track to the Animal!

(answer key)

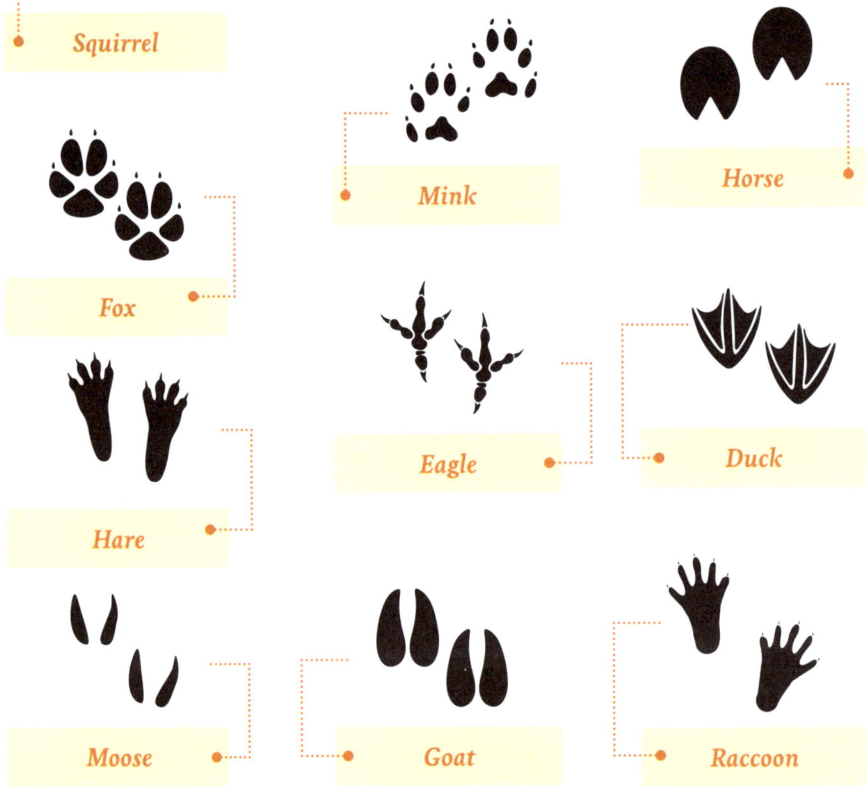

Fox	*Mink*	*Duck*	*Squirrel*	*Goat*
Hare	*Horse*	*Eagle*	*Raccoon*	*Moose*

Complete the Image

solution on page 162

solution on page 162

solution on page 163

solution on page 163

solution on page 164

solution on page 165

solution on page 166

solution on page 167

solution on page 167

"There is nothing so American as our national parks.... The fundamental idea behind the parks...is that the country belongs to the people... for the enrichment of the lives of all of us."

President Franklin D. Roosevelt

"What a country chooses to save is what a country chooses to say about itself."

Mollie Beattie; director of the U.S. Fish and Wildlife Service, 1993–1996

STAY WILD
GET OUTSIDE
N
ADVENTURE BEGINS HERE
W
E
S
OUTDOOR ADVENTURES
THE MOUNTAINS ARE CALLING
UT
US
RAFTING ADVENTURE
SINCE '90
OUTDOOR ADVENTURE
CAMPING CLUB
TAKE A HIKE
Rafting
ADVENTURE
SUMMER CAMP

"The idea of preserving in a national grouping such spots of scenic beauty and historic memory originated here in this country... Other countries have followed our pioneering example and set aside their most magnificent scenic areas as national treasures for the enjoyment of present and future generations."

President Dwight D. Eisenhower

HAPPY CAMPER

"If you drive to [a National Park], you'll get some appreciation for the scale and beauty of the outdoors. When you walk into it, then you... discover it in a much slower, more majestic sort of way."

Bill Bryson, travel author/journalist

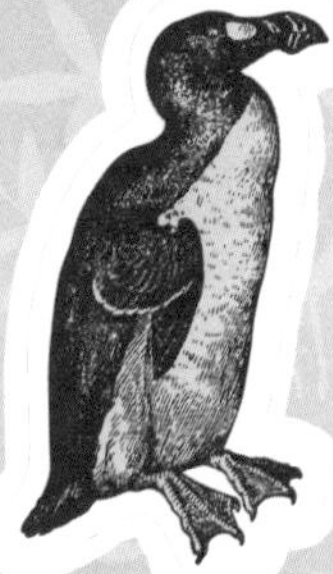

Match the Animal to the Park!

Some national parks draw visitors hoping to spot certain key animals. How many animals can you match to their signature parks?

Sea Turtle

Mountain Goat

Nēnē

Bison

Brown Bear

Carlsbad Caverns (New Mexico)

Yellowstone (Wyoming)

Katmai (Alaska)

Glacier (Montana)

White Sands (New Mexico)

Hawai'i Volcanoes

Everglades (Florida)

Theodore Roosevelt (North Dakota)

Virgin Islands

Pinnacles (California)

Bat

Horse

Condor

Roadrunner

Alligator

answers on the next page

Match the Animal to the Park!

(answer key)

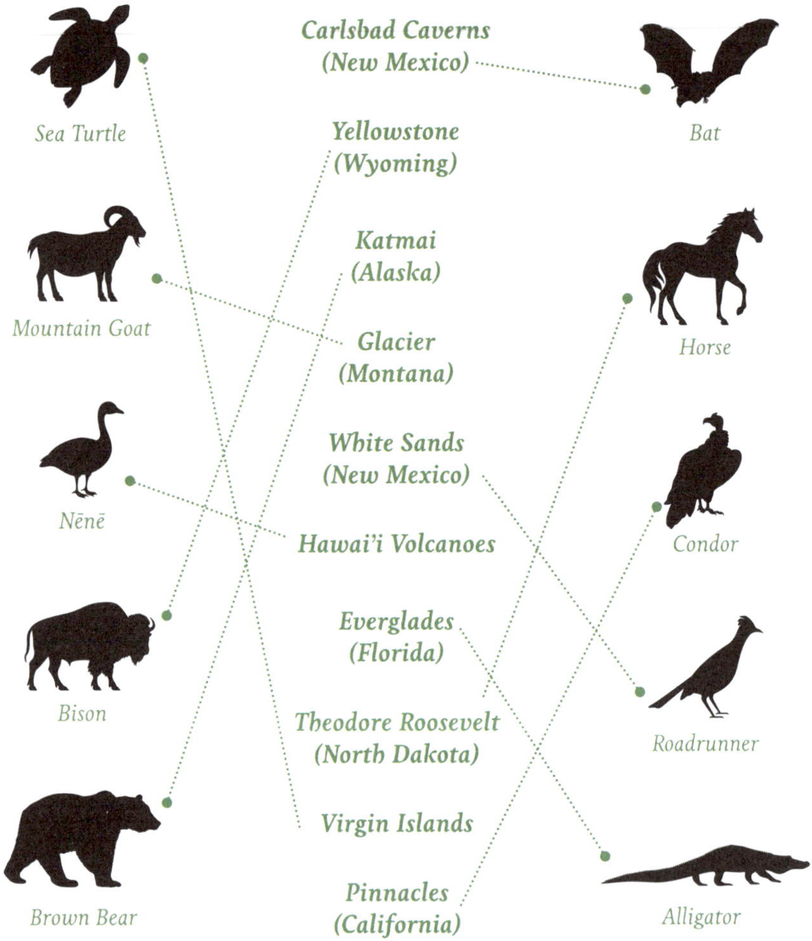

answers on the next page

Let's Embroider a National Park!

Embroidery is a wonderful way to preserve the beauty of a national park's scenery. If you can thread a needle, you can embroider.

What you'll need:

- Water-soluble fabric pen
- Smooth cotton fabric
- Embroidery needle
- Embroidery hoop
- 4 colors of 6-stranded, cotton DMC embroidery floss
- Motif

What you'll do:

1. Make a photocopy of the arch motif and tape it to a window, which will act as a light box. Tape your fabric over the design and trace with the water-soluble pen.

2. Cut thread about 16 inches (40 cm) long. Divide it into the number of strands you need at one end, then slide a finger between the strands and down the length of the thread to separate them.

3. If you're unfamiliar with the types of stitches, search online for how to do straight stitch and backstitch, plus how to tie off.

Arches National Park

As one of the most popular national parks, Arches is home to more than 2,000 natural red sandstone formations such as pinnacles, towers, rock fins, balanced rocks, and, of course, arches. Delicate Arch is a 52-foot-tall (15.8 m) freestanding natural arch, the largest and most famous in the park.

DMC 310

DMC 3857

DMC 420

DMC 169

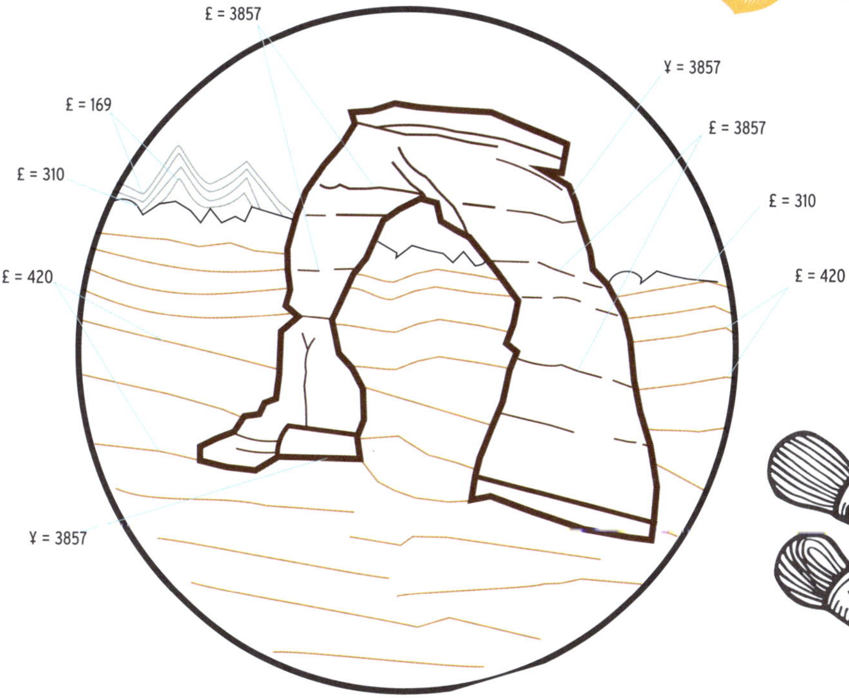

¥ = chain stitch £ = backstitch

1. Chain stitch the outline of the arch using three strands of DMC 3857 floss.
2. Backstitch the arch details using two strands of DMC 3857 floss.
3. Backstitch terrain using two strands of DMC 420 floss.
4. Backstitch horizon using two strands of DMC 310 floss.
5. Backstitch mountain caps usign two strands of DMC 169 floss.

Let's Go Birding!

Because of their protected land status, the national parks and sites are an incredible haven for birds—and birdwatchers. One reason for the large variety of species is because the park system spans tropical, temperate, mountain, desert, and arctic climate zones, and therefore has birds characteristic of each.

When trying to determine which bird you're seeing, keep in mind that in addition to bird calls, experienced birders observe a bird's size, shape, and behavior. Is it a large bird, or small? Is it slim and elegant, or heavy and lumbering? Does it have a round body, short tail, long neck, spoon bill? Does it hop, glide, dart, soar, swim, or hang upside down from a branch?

Here are some terms birders use to pinpoint colors, in an attempt to scrutinize more than the readily obvious (e.g., "white patch on top of the head").

- ○ Bill
- ○ Throat
- ○ Breast
- ○ Belly
- ○ Crown
- ○ Nape
- ○ Rump
- ○ Wingtip
- ○ Tail feathers

As you become more comfortable with looking at bird characteristics, you'll begin to refine what you see and your language for describing it. Is the feather plain brown, dark brown, or streaked brown? Is the throat red, pink, or blush? Is the white patch on the throat or breast, and is it more buff than white?

Next to a good pair of binoculars, one of a birder's best tools is the logbook. Important things to note include the date, time, and location of where you saw the bird. You might include a note about the weather or something about the habitat or its behavior. If you can, identify whether it's male or female, jot down what its song or call sounds like, or include a little sketch. Here's a sample birder's log:

Date	*Time*	*Location*	*Weather*	*Species*	*Notes & Obstervations*

Match the Track to the Animal!

Of course you don't need to visit an official national park to see wild animals—in fact, sometimes a park's signature animals are rarely seen. But they do leave behind tracks. See how many you can match.

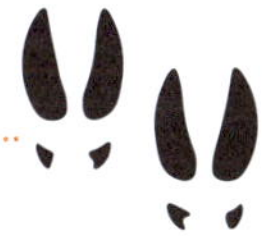

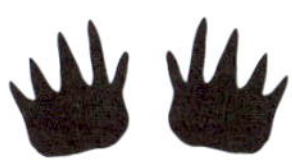

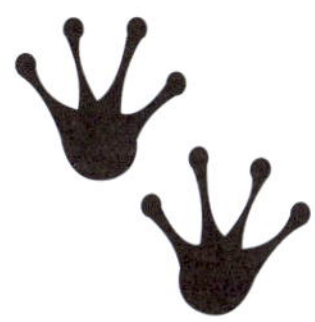

Lynx	Frog	Porcupine	Turtle	Bear
Rabbit	Lizard	Wolf	Mink	Deer

answers on the next page

Match the Track to the Animal!

(answer key)

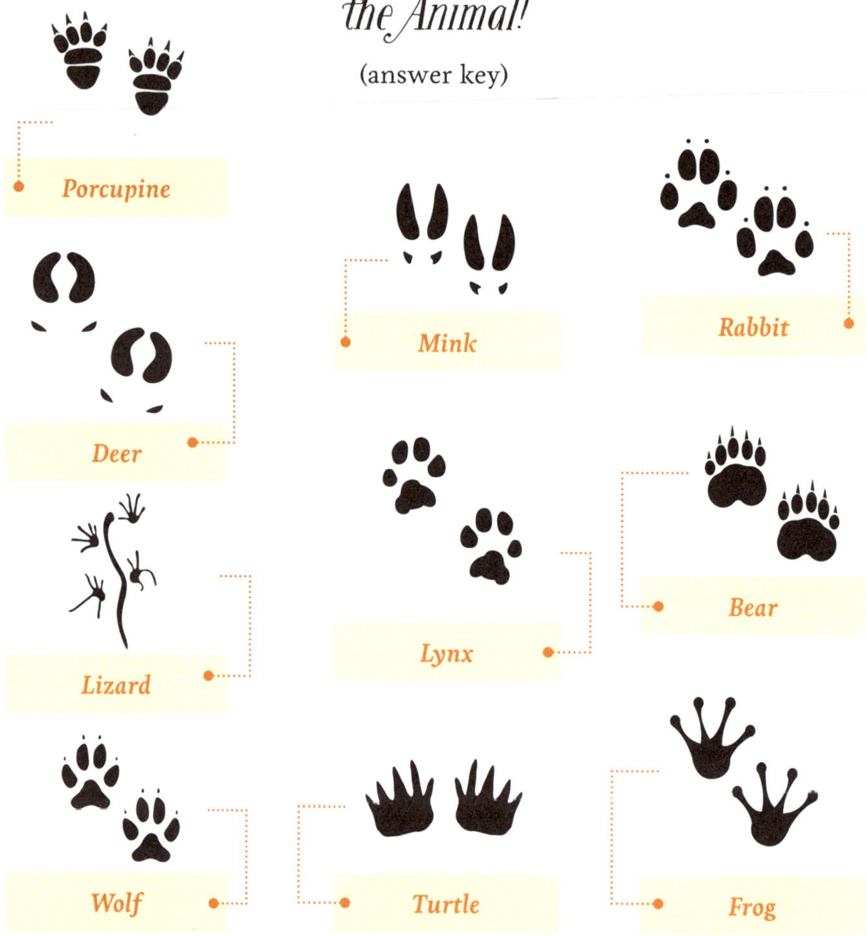

Lynx	Frog	Porcupine	Turtle	Bear
Rabbit	Lizard	Wolf	Mink	Deer

Caption This!

Test Your Geography!

Some national historic sites and monuments are easy to place (hello, White House and Statue of Liberty!), but how good are you at finding some of the others?

- *Gettysburg NMP*
- *Mount Rushmore N MEM*
- *Stonewall NM*
- *Craters of the Moon NM & PRES*
- *Golden Gate NRA*
- *Lewis and Clark NHP*
- *St. Croix Island NHS*
- *Harpers Ferry NHP*
- *Apostle Islands NL*
- *Crocodile Lake NWR*
- *Little Rock Central High School NHS*
- *Petroglyph NM*
- *Rio Grande WSR*
- *Mojave N PRES*
- *Dinosaur NM*

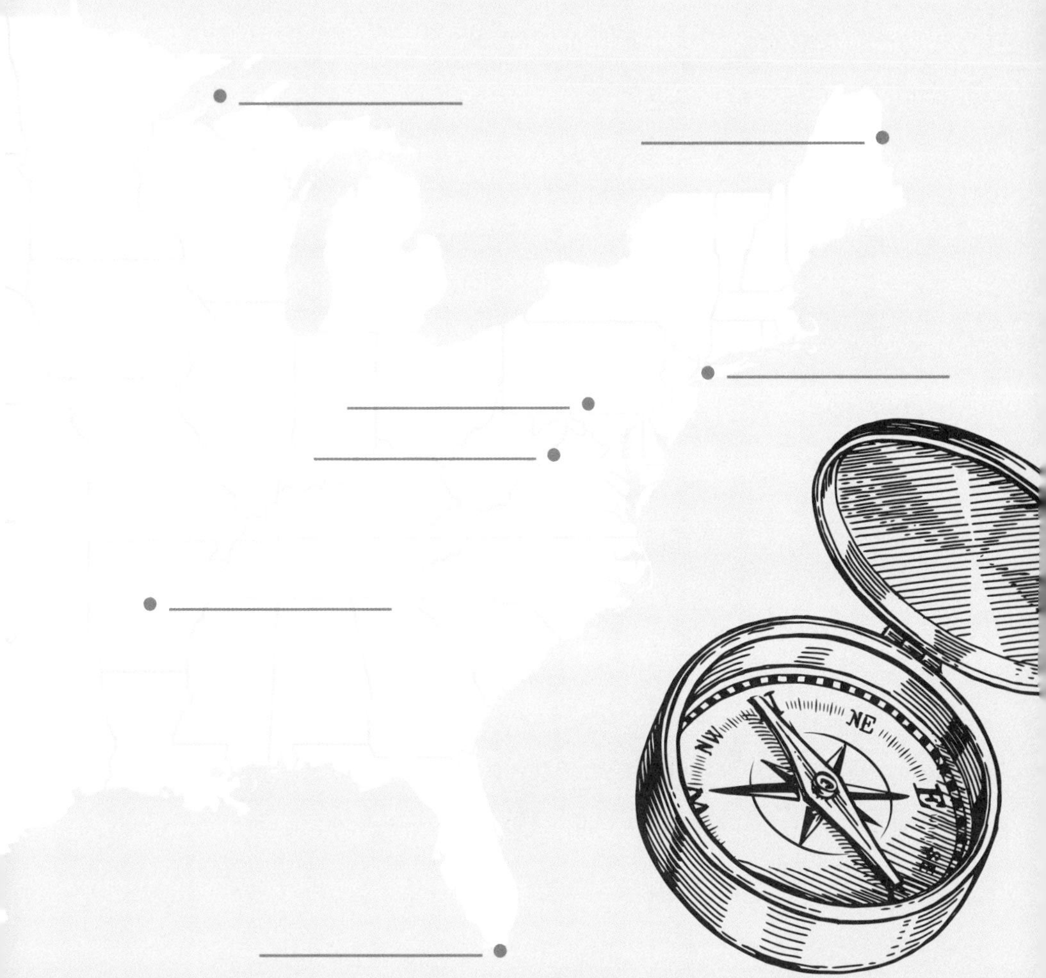

answers on page 168

They Said What?!

Even the NPS craves reviews online. There's been a trend, however, of people posting (dare we say) ridiculous negative reviews. These reviews have ended up on postcards, posters, and calendars as "subpar parks," and even the NPS enjoys posting them to social media. Here are some examples of 1-star reviews:

"Scenery is not breathtaking." (Yosemite NP)

"There wasn't a single pickleball court in sight." (Hawai'i Volcanoes NP)

"A very, very large hole." (Grand Canyon NP)

"It's basically just a lot of sand." (Great Sand Dunes NP)

"It wasn't that entertaining." (Shenandoah NP)

"Most of the different formations looked redundant." (Zion NP)

Now, have some fun and take a turn making up your own subpar, 1-star reviews of these famous national sites.

Jefferson Memorial

Misty Fjords NM

Devils Tower NM

Trivia I

What was the first official National Park, established in 1872?

- O Yosemite
- O Yellowstone
- O Mount Rushmore
- O Grand Canyon

When was the National Park Service established?

- O 1871
- O 1900
- O 1963
- O 1916

Which state has the most official national parks?

- O California
- O Alaska
- O Utah
- O Colorado

How many national parks, monuments, and historic sites are in the United States (as of 2024)?

- O 185
- O 63
- O 430
- O 346

Which national park is situated entirely south of the equator?

- O Virgin Islands National Park
- O National Park of American Samoa
- O Everglades National Park
- O Channel Islands National Park

Which of the following is NOT one of the 19 "designated names" or units in the National Park System?

- O National Mountain Peak
- O National Military Park
- O National Recreation Area
- O National Lakeshore

answers on page 174

"Today, across our land, the National Park System represents America at its best."

Geroge B. Hartzog, Jr., NPS Director 1964–1972

INDIANA DUNES NATIONAL PARK
ISLE ROYALE NATIONAL PARK
VOYAGEURS NATIONAL PARK
GATEWAY ARCH NATIONAL PARK
CUYAHOGA VALLEY NATIONAL PARK
BISCAYNE NATIONAL PARK
DRY TORTUGAS NATIONAL PARK
EVERGLADES NATIONAL PARK

MAMMOTH CAVE NATIONAL PARK
CONGAREE NATIONAL PARK
GREAT SMOKY MOUNTAINS NATIONAL PARK
VIRGIN ISLANDS NATIONAL PARK
SHENANDOAH NATIONAL PARK
NEW RIVER GORGE NATIONAL PARK & PRESERVE
ACADIA NATIONAL PARK

"We have agreed not to drive our automobiles into cathedrals, concert halls, art museums... and the other sanctums of our culture; we should treat our national parks with the same deference, for they, too, are holy places."

Edward Abbey, Desert Solitaire

GLACIER
NATIONAL PARK
THEODORE
ROOSEVELT
NATIONAL PARK
BADLANDS
NATIONAL PARK
WIND CAVE
NATIONAL PARK
ARCHES
NATIONAL PARK
BRYCE CANYON
NATIONAL PARK
CANYONLANDS
NATIONAL PARK
CAPITOL REEF
NATIONAL PARK

ZION
NATIONAL
PARK
GRAND
TETON
NATIONAL PARK
YELLOWSTONE
NATIONAL PARK
HOT SPRINGS
NATIONAL PARK
CARLSBAD
CAVERNS
NATIONAL PARK
WHITE SANDS
NATIONAL PARK
BIG BEND
NATIONAL PARK
GUADALUPE
MOUNTAINS
NATIONAL PARK

"National parks and reserves are an integral aspect of intelligent use of natural resources... thus ensuring that future generations may know the majesty of the earth as we know it today."

President John F. Kennedy

DEATH VALLEY NATIONAL PARK
JOSHUA TREE NATIONAL PARK
KINGS CANYON NATIONAL PARK
LASSEN VOLCANIC NATIONAL PARK
PINNACLES NATIONAL PARK
REDWOODS NATIONAL & STATE PARKS
SEQUOIA NATIONAL PARK
YOSEMITE NATIONAL PARK

HALEAKALĀ
NATIONAL PARK
HAWAI'I
VOLCANOES
NATIONAL PARK
GREAT
BASIN
NATIONAL PARK
NATIONAL PARK OF
AMERICAN
SAMOA
BLACK
CANYON
OF THE
GUNNISON
NATIONAL PARK
GREAT SAND
DUNES
NATIONAL PARK
& PRESERVE
MESA VERDE
NATIONAL PARK
ROCKY
MOUNTAIN
NATIONAL PARK

"In wilderness is the
preservation of the world."

Henry David Thoreau, author

DENALI
NATIONAL PARK
& PRESERVE
GATES OF
THE ARCTIC
NATIONAL PARK
& PRESERVE
GLACIER BAY
NATIONAL PARK
& PRESERVE
KATMAI
NATIONAL PARK
& PRESERVE
KENAI FJORDS
NATIONAL PARK
KOBUK
VALLEY
NATIONAL
PARK
LAKE CLARK
NATIONAL PARK
& PRESERVE
WRANGLL-
ST. ELIAS
NATIONAL PARK
& PRESERVE

CRATER LAKE NATIONAL PARK
MOUNT RAINER NATIONAL PARK
NORTH CASCADES NATIONAL PARK
OLYMPIC NATIONAL PARK
GRAND CANYON NATIONAL PARK
PETRIFIED FOREST NATIONAL PARK
SAGUARO NATIONAL PARK
CHANNEL ISLANDS NATIONAL PARK

ARCHES NATIONAL PARK, UTAH

SAGUARO NATIONAL PARK, ARIZONA

GRAND TETON NATIONAL PARK, WYOMING

SEQUOIA NATIONAL PARK, CALIFORNIA

LASSEN VOLCANIC NATIONAL PARK, CALIFORNIA

MOUNT RAINIER NATIONAL PARK, WASHINGTON

OLYMPIA NATIONAL PARK, WASHINGTON

REDWOODS NATIONAL PARK, CALIFORNIA

“The National Park System also provides, through areas that are significant in history and prehistory, a physical as well as spiritual linking of present-day Americans with the past of their country.”

Newton B. Drury, NPS Director, 1940–1951

"Our National Parks belong to each of us, and they are natural places to learn, exercise, volunteer, spend time with family and friends, and enjoy the magnificent beauty of our great land."

President George W. Bush

CAMPING
ADVENTURE

"National parks are the
best idea we ever had.
Absolutely American,
absolutely democratic,
they reflect us at our best
rather than our worst."

Wallace Stegner, author

"The parks do not belong to one state or to one section.... they belong as much to the man of Massachusetts, of Michigan, of Florida, as they do to the people of California, of Wyoming, and of Arizona."

Stephen T. Mather, NPS Director, 1917–1929

Caption This!

Match the Sticker!

answers on page 170

What Is Your *National Park Name?*

Match the first letter of your first or last name with the first list of words. Match your birthday with the second list. Be sure to add a type of park, monument, or historic site (refer to the list on page 4). Now you have your national park or site name!

Presenting:

____

____

____

A Amazing
B Breathtaking
C Cosmic
D Dazzling
E Exciting
F Fabulous
G Grand
H Handsome
I Invigorating
J Joyous
K Kaleidoscopic
L Lofty
M Magnificent
N Noble
O Opulent
P Plenty
Q Quirky
R Regal
S Sublime
T Thrilling
U Upbeat
V Vast
W Wondrous
X Xeric
Y Youthful
Z Zesty

1 Climbs
2 Scenery
3 Rivers
4 Hikes
5 Glaciers
6 Woods
7 Vistas
8 Plateau
9 Springs
10 Trails
11 Sights
12 Caves
13 Birds
14 Wildflowers
15 Waves
16 Stones
17 Lighthouse
18 Lakes
19 Wildlife
20 Sunsets
21 Stargazing
22 Views
23 Bouldering
24 Waterfalls
25 Camping
26 Forts
27 Hills
28 Fossils
29 Trees
30 Volcano
31 Sands

Let's Go Stargazing!

You don't need a telescope or even binoculars to view the stars. Sometimes it's as easy as turning off the lights and heading into your backyard. However, some places are better than others for viewing.

As of 2024, there were 145 designated Dark Sky locations across the United States, as awarded by the International Dark-Sky Association (IDSA); 17 of them were official national parks. These areas are spectacular for minimal or zero light pollution, and they often host star parties, astronomy festivals, and even astrophotography workshops.

The idea of protecting the night sky might sound strange, but darkness supports light-sensitive wildlife and, in turn, their ecosystems. Animals such as big cats, owls, and rodents depend on darkness to hunt, mate, and avoid other predators; artificial light can interfere with their vision and affect their ability to hunt or forage. Amazingly, many birds navigate by the stars, and night-lit buildings can steer them off course. Sea turtle hatchlings rely on the moon to direct them toward the ocean, and busy nearby highways can draw them toward these dangerous roads. Decreased darkness can also affect the hormones, thermoregulation, and reproduction of amphibians. Even zooplankton try to avoid excessive light: instead of surfacing at night, where animals that subsist on them can find them, they stay deeper under water in areas of intense night light. Humans, too, need darkness to maintain our circadian rhythms and get enough rest.

You don't have to visit a national park or official Dark Sky park to see the stars.

Here are some tips for viewing a dark(er) sky near you:

- Choose a clear night with the smallest-phase moon; a full moon will obscure shooting stars (meteor showers).
- Go as late at night as possible for the darkest sky; pre-dawn is best for seeing meteors.
- Dress appropriately and comfortably; you won't want to stay outside very long if the temperature drops!
- Bring a blanket, something hot to drink, and some snacks.
- Get away from artificial light; light pollution comes not just from city buildings and streetlamps but also porch lights, lighting from inside homes, and your phone.
- Use a red flashlight or headlamp, if needed.
- Give your eyes 30 minutes to adjust to the darkness; let them adapt by not looking at your phone.
- Study what you can readily see, such as the moon or the Milky Way, and look for shooting stars (meteors).
- To pick out constellations, there are many apps that allow you to point your phone toward the sky and it will tell you what's up there. (Pre-download it so you're not looking at a bright screen.)

Meteor Showers of Note

- ○ Quadrantids (January)
- ○ Lyrids (April)
- ○ Eta Aquarids (May)
- ○ Perseids (August)
- ○ Orionids (October)
- ○ Leonids (November)
- ○ Geminids (December)

Celestial Signposts

When you don't have a compass to point you due north, you can still get your bearings from the sun. No matter where you are, the sun always rises in the east and sets in the west. However, the sun isn't the only star that can help you find your way home. For centuries, travelers have used the night sky to chart their course, whether on land or on the sea.

North Star: Polaris is known as the North Star because its celestial location is in near-perfect alignment with the North Pole. This means that, as the Earth turns, Polaris seems to be the only star locked in place in the night sky (at least in the Northern Hemisphere). Polaris is a bright star located in the tail of the Little Dipper (Ursa Minor) constellation. The easiest way to locate it is to find the Big Dipper (Ursa Major) and follow a straight line up from the two stars on the outer edge of the dipper's cup. Those pointer stars will lead you right to Polaris—and Polaris will lead you north!

Orion: Orion is a constellation that is easy to find and extremely helpful to use as a navigation tool. Orion's most distinguishing feature is its "belt," a straight line of three bright stars that run across the middle of its hourglass shape. The belt runs roughly east to west in the sky, but another line of stars that make up the "sword" that hangs below Orion's belt point to due south on the horizon. Orion may not be as readily visible in the Northern Hemisphere during the summer months due to the angle of the Earth on its axis.

How Many Constellations Do You Know?

Most of the sky's constellations got their names from ancient Greek, Roman, and Middle Eastern cultures and their stories about gods, goddesses, and animals. Those on this page aren't all in the northern sky at the same time, but how many can you name?

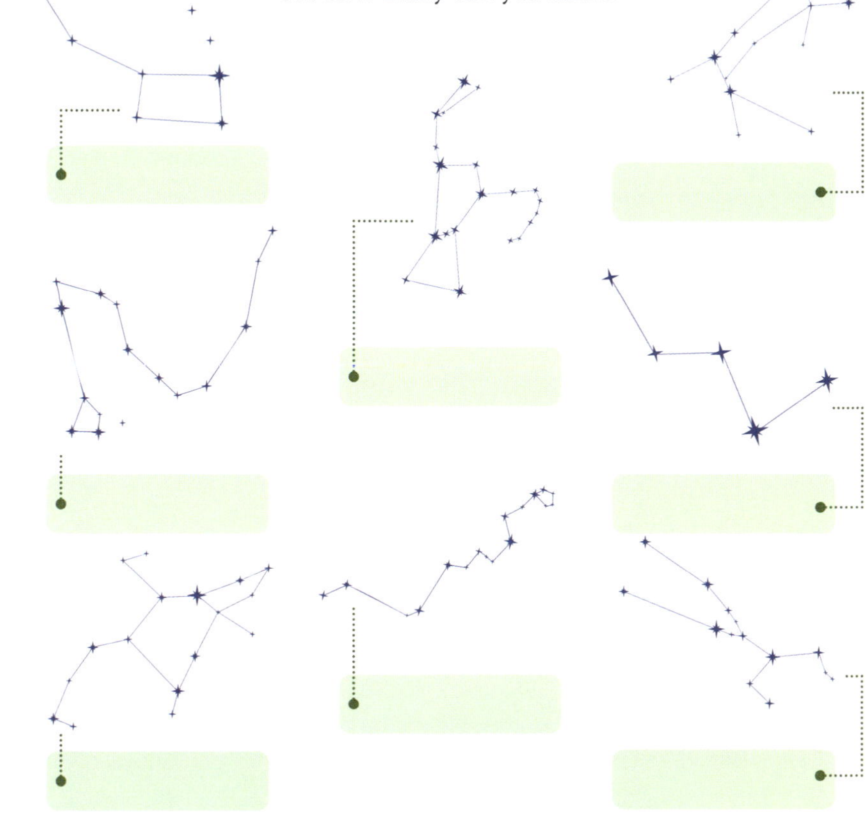

Orion ***Ursa Minor*** ***Taurus*** ***Draco***

Cassiopeia ***Canis Major*** ***Hydra*** ***Perseus***

answers on the next page

How Many Constellations Do You Know?

(answer key)

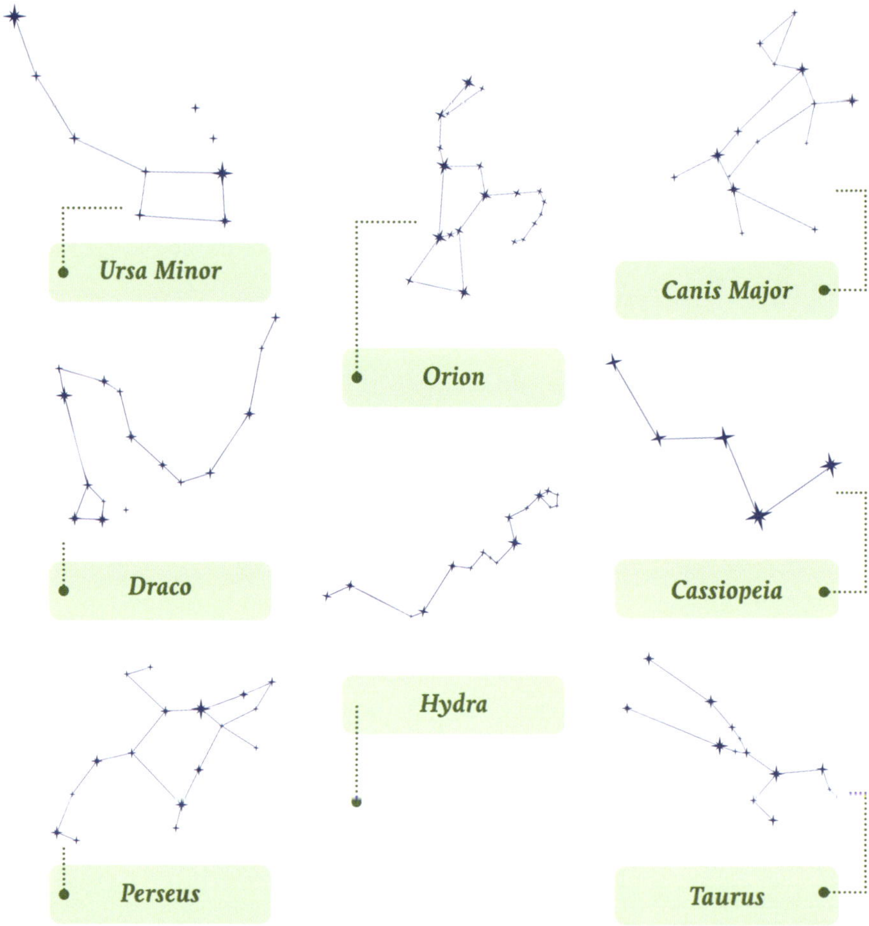

Orion	Ursa Minor	Taurus	Draco
Cassiopeia	Canis Major	Hydra	Perseus

Let's Go Geocaching!

If you've never heard of it before, think of geocaching ("GEO-kash-ing") as a worldwide scavenger hunt. Put another way, it's an outdoor treasure-hunting adventure that's happening at any given time anywhere around the world. There are millions of them in nearly every country!

To get started, create an account on any of the geocache sites or download a geocaching app. This is where you will find a geocache's GPS coordinates. (You might just find one near you right now!) Once you have the coordinates and general location, it's off on a hike you go. Sometimes your trek will take you along a babbling creek; sometimes you'll have to scramble some boulders; sometimes, it's just a walk down your street.

What are you looking for? Typically, there's a small weatherproof box or case that contains a tiny logbook and pencil. Look high and low, behind rocks, and up in trees (but not too high up). Sign your name or initials with the date, and put it back as you found it. Depending on the size of the case, there might be a trade or swag item (pins, trinkets, marbles, keychains, pretty rocks or seashells). The general rule of thumb is that if you take something, leave something.

Part of the fun of geocaching is sharing your experience with others! In addition to signing the logbook, many 'cachers log their experience online. There's also an International Geocaching Day in August where you can join the global geocaching community. Now get out there and find your next hidden treasure!

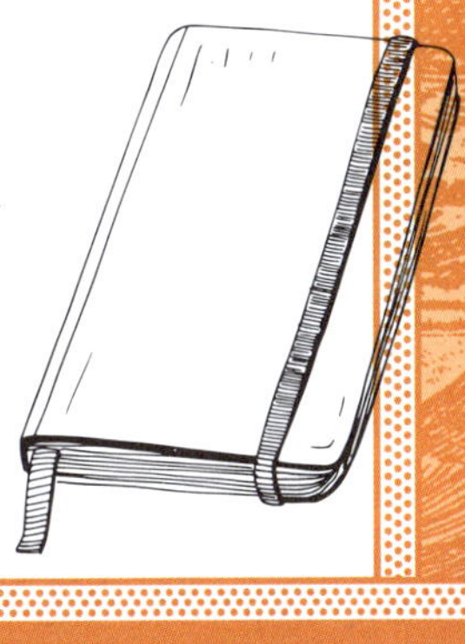

Pitching a Tarp

You might already have a tent. These portable forms of shelter offer easy-to-assemble protection from the elements. There are dozens of types of tents out there—ridge, pyramid, dome, pop-up, tunnel, etc.—each with its own benefits. But assuming you weren't planning on staying overnight...read on.

It's okay if you don't have an elaborate store-bought tent that instantly assembles itself. With a tarp, rope or paracord, and a few well-placed sticks, you can create your own tent in no time at all. Just follow these simple steps:

Step 1: Use the clove hitch (see page 109) to tie the rope (or a line of paracord or wire) between two trees. If you can't find two trees close enough together, find two sturdy branches and drive them into the ground to use as upright poles. (The closer your shelter's center line is to the ground, the more coverage it will provide.)

Step 2: Drape the tarp over the line, so that the tarp is folded in half.

Step 3: Stretching the tarp out to create an "A-frame" shape, weigh down the corners of your tarp with heavy rocks or logs.

Know your Knots

There are hundreds of different ways to tie a knot, but the two pictured here are some of the most useful and effective in a survival situation.

The **bowline** (BO-lin) creates a loop at the end of a rope that won't change size or slip. You can tie it around yourself—or another person—in a rescue situation.

Step 1: Create a loop in the left side of the rope (top over bottom).

Step 2: Feed the right strand up through the loop.

Step 3: Bring the right strand around the back of the left strand and feed it down into the loop. Tighten!

The **clove hitch** is a quick, easy knot that can secure your line to a post, tree, or carabiner.

Step 1: Wrap the rope around an object, then bring the rope around a second time above the first wrap.

Step 2: As you bring the rope around to the front, feed it through the loop you just created.

Step 3: Tighten by pulling hard on the two strands, being sure to push the two loops together.

Spot the 10 Differences!

solution on page 161

Complete the Image

"The establishment of the National Park Service is justified by considerations of... the value of natural beauty as a National asset, and of the effectiveness of outdoor life and recreation in the production of good citizenship."

President Theodore Roosevelt

FIND YOUR WILD
Go Outside
TAKE ME TO THE DESERT
LIFE IS BETTER
OUTSIDE
STAY WILD
NEVER STOP
EXPLORING
LIFE'S SHORT
GO OUTSIDE
STAY WILD
OUTDOOR
ADVENTURE
EXPLORE
THE UNSEEN
GET LOST
FLY HIGH

"I went to the woods because I wished to live deliberately, to front only the essential facts of life, and see if I could not learn what it had to teach, and not, when I came to die, discover that I had not lived."

Hendry David Thoreau, Walden

"Such great national symbols and meccas... and numerous other treasures of our national park system belong to all of us, both legally and spiritually. These tangible evidences of our cultural and natural heritage help make us all Americans."

Edwin C. Bearss,
NPS Chief Historian, 1981–1994

ADVENTURE
BEGINS HERE
Hiking
IS MY THERAPY
WILD & FREE
CAMPING
WILD&FREE
RAFTING
LIFE IS GOOD. FULL STREAM AHEAD
RAFTING
Say Yes to Adventure
SAY Yes! TO
ADVENTURE
CAMPING
FOREST
MOUNTAINS
WATER WARRIOR

HIKING
CLUB
KAYAK & CANOE
ADVENTURE
TAKE
A HIKE
HAPPY CAMPER
MOUNTAIN
CA
ADVENTURES
US
OUTDOOR EXPEDITION
Go Outside
THE
Great
Outdoors
U.S.A.

"The truth is, national monuments and parks are part of the identity... as a people. They are more than natural wonders; they're the birthright we pass from generation to generation — a birthright of every American. And preserving them is the fulfillment of a promise to our children and all those who will come to leave this world a little better than we found it."

President Joseph R. Biden

Caption This!

Match the Sticker!

answers on page 172

Sudoku

			9				6	7
	9					2		8
4	6			7	8			
3	2			9	4		7	
7			6		3			2
	1		7	8			4	3
			8	5			1	6
5		1					9	
6	7				9			

solution on page 176

Trivia II

What is skijoring?

- ○ A sport where a person on a sled is pulled by dogs
- ○ A sport where a person cross-country skis, periodically stopping to shoot at a target
- ○ A sport where a person on skis is pulled by horses, dogs, or a snowmobile
- ○ A sport where a person skis over a frozen lake

Which national park has its own commercial airport?

- ○ Grand Teton (Wyoming)
- ○ Denali (Alaska)
- ○ Glacier (Montana)
- ○ Arches (Utah)

Which national park can be reached only by boat or aircraft?

- ○ Katmai (Alaska)
- ○ Dry Tortugas (Florida)
- ○ Isle Royale (Michigan)
- ○ All of the above

As of 2024, which of the following was NOT part of the National Park system?

- ○ Castle Hill Lighthouse (Rhode Island)
- ○ Historic U.S. Highway 66
- ○ Alcatraz Island (California)
- ○ Brooklyn Bridge (New York)

What is the most visited national monument?

- ○ Muir Woods (California
- ○ Devils Tower (Wyoming)
- ○ Statue of Liberty (New York
- ○ Grand Staircase-Escalante (Utah)

Which of the following national parks does NOT have sand dunes?

- ○ Death Valley (California)
- ○ Kobuk Valley (Alaska)
- ○ Indiana Dunes (Indiana)
- ○ Great Basin (Nevada)

answers on page 175

Sudoku

				1				
9					3	4		8
6	7		5				2	1
			1	3		7	8	
	1	5				2	4	
	4	7		6	5			
7	5				6		1	4
1		2	4					9
				9				

solution on page 176

When Was the Park Founded?

It's been more than 150 years since the first national park was established. See if you can match the year to when each of the parks below was founded. As a clue, each park's tagline is included next to the year.

_____ Biscayne
_____ Canyonlands
_____ Congaree
_____ Crater Lake
_____ Cuyahoga Valley
_____ Grand Teton
_____ Great Basin
_____ Great Smoky Mountains
_____ Haleakalā
_____ Hot Springs
_____ Mammoth Cave
_____ Mesa Verde
_____ New River Gorge
_____ Olympic
_____ Redwood
_____ Saguaro
_____ Voyageurs
_____ Zion

A. 1929 (Mountains of the Imagination)
B. 1921 (Where History and Nature Meet)
C. 1916 (A Rare and Sacred Landscape)
D. 1986 (From Caves to the Cosmos)
E. 1906 (A Sacred Place)
F. 1938 (Discover Diverse Wilderness)
G. 1968 (So Much More Than the Tallest Trees)
H. 1974 (A River Renewed)
I. 1980 (A Watery Wonderland)
J. 1994 (Icon of the Southwest)
K. 1941 (More Than a Cave)
L. 1940 (A Wondrous Diversity of Life)
M. 1919 (Utah's First National Park)
N. 2020 (A River Runs through It)
O. 1964 (A Lifetime of Exploration Awaits)
P. 2003 (Home of Champions)
Q. 1975 (A Park of Water, Islands, and Horizons)
R. 1902 (Deep Water in a Sleeping Volcano)

answers on the next page

When Was the Park Founded?

(answer key)

I Biscayne
O Canyonlands
P Congaree
R Crater Lake
H Cuyahoga Valley
A Grand Teton
D Great Basin
L Great Smoky Mountains
C Haleakalā
B Hot Springs
K Mammoth Cave
E Mesa Verde
N New River Gorge
F Olympic
G Redwood
J Saguaro
Q Voyageurs
M Zion

A. 1929 (Mountains of the Imagination)
B. 1921 (Where History and Nature Meet)
C. 1916 (A Rare and Sacred Landscape)
D. 1986 (From Caves to the Cosmos)
E. 1906 (A Sacred Place)
F. 1938 (Discover Diverse Wilderness)
G. 1968 (So Much More Than the Tallest Trees)
H. 1974 (A River Renewed)
I. 1980 (A Watery Wonderland)
J. 1994 (Icon of the Southwest)
K. 1941 (More Than a Cave)
L. 1940 (A Wondrous Diversity of Life)
M. 1919 (Utah's First National Park)
N. 2020 (A River Runs through It)
O. 1964 (A Lifetime of Exploration Awaits)
P. 2003 (Home of Champions)
Q. 1975 (A Park of Water, Islands, and Horizons)
R. 1902 (Deep Water in a Sleeping Volcano)

Make and Take a Snack!

What's a trip to a scenic park, without something to nosh? Be it GORP ("good ol' raisins and peanuts") or a full-out picnic, the only thing that limits you is how much you're willing to carry.

A small charcuterie box is a cute and portable snack/meal that's packed with protein, fat, and calories to help you avoid the hangries and get the most out of your nature viewing. Many of the items are shelf stable (nuts, crackers, bread, cookies, candy) or can go without refrigeration for a small amount of time (fruit, some cheeses and cured meats, pickled items). Turn the page for some inspiration. Just be sure that what you pack in, you also pack out. One of the mottos of the NPS is *leave no trace*.

Charcuterie A-Go-Go

Serves 4 to 6 people • Use a 9-inch (23 cm) square cake box

What you'll need:

- ½ cup (120 g) whole grain mustard
- ¼ cup (85 g) honey
- ½ cup (65 g) cornichons
- 4-ounce (113 g) log cranberry and cinnamon goat cheese
- 8 ounces (227 g) thinly sliced Genoa salami, divided
- 8 ounces (227 g) Manchego, half cubed and half left in a wedge
- 8 ounces (227 g) seedless green grapes
- ½ cup (75 g) blueberries
- 8 ounces (227 g) seedless red grapes
- 2 strawberries
- ½ cup (70 g) Marcona almonds
- 1/3 cup (50 g) pistachios
- 3/4 cup (105 g) raw almonds
- 1/3 cup (45 g) dried apricots
- 1/3 cup (50 g) chocolate-covered almonds
- 2 chocolate-covered toffees with nuts
- Flowers, to decorate

What you'll do:

1. Fill three 2-ounce (60 ml) jars or bowls with mustard, honey, and cornichons and place in a triangle starting at the bottom center of the box and finishing in the center.
2. Slice the goat cheese, shingle the slices, and place between the jars in the center.

3. Make the salami rose. Cut one slice of Genoa salami in half, and with the cut side facing down, roll it into a spiral. Pinch the base between two fingers and use the other half to wrap around it, slightly higher than the first. Continue wrapping half of the Genoa salami pieces around the core, each subsequent piece slightly higher than the last. If necessary, secure the base with a toothpick, then place upright in the box above the goat cheese.
4. Place the Manchego wedge in the bottom-right corner of the box. Place a few cubes in front and the remaining cubes in the top-left corner.
5. Fill the remaining opposing corners with the green and red grapes.
6. With the remaining salami and chorizo slices, create loose bundles using four slices for each. Working one at a time, shingle two slices and fold in half, then repeat with two more slices, tucking the four slices together. Transfer the bundles to the box before making more, securing with toothpicks if necessary.
7. Fill in any gaps with the blueberries, strawberries, Marcona almonds, pistachios, raw almonds, dried apricots, chocolate almonds, and chocolate toffees.
8. Decorate with flowers.

Meat Lovers' Board

Serves 6 people • Use a 10 x 12-inch (25 x 30 cm) board

What you'll need:

- 4 ounces (115 g) thinly sliced prosciutto
- 4 ounces (115 g) thinly sliced bresaola
- 15 mini salami sticks
- 2 (8-ounce) rounds Brie
- 1 small goat cheese round
- 1 small goat cheese square
- 4 ounces (115 g) saucisson, sliced
- 4 ounces (115 g) thinly sliced Genoa salami
- Mixed nuts, plus more to serve
- 3 caper berries
- Fresh herbs, to garnish
- Whole grain mustard, to serve
- Veggie chips, to serve
- Green olives, to serve

What you'll do:

1. Working one slice at a time, create a loose, overlapping line of prosciutto down the center of the board by gently twisting and folding the slices as you transfer them to the board. Repeat with the bresaola, filling the bottom right corner of the board.
2. Fill the bottom-left and top-right corners with the salami sticks. Place the two small bries on the top right side of the board, one propped up against the other. Place the small round goat cheese in the top left corner of the board and the square goat cheese bottom-center.
3. Fill the top left side of the board with the saucisson, allowing the

slices to overlap in a pile. Then fold the salami slices into quarters and shingle down the remaining space on the left side of the board. Fill in any gaps with mixed nuts, caper berries, and fresh herbs.

4. Serve with whole grain mustard, veggie chips, green olives, and extra nuts on the side.

Fruit and Nut Forward

Serves 4 • Use a 12-inch (30 cm) round cake box

What you'll need:

- ½ cup (68 g) hazelnuts
- ½ cup (65 g) salted cashews
- ½ cup (75 g) blueberries
- 3 large, colorful, and ripe pears, thinly sliced
- 6 ounces (170 g) Stilton, broken into pieces
- ½ cup (70 g) toasted almonds
- Fresh mint sprigs, to garnish

What you'll do:

1. Place the hazelnuts, cashews, and most of the blueberries in bowls and place in a triangular shape at the edges of the box.
2. Shingle the pear slices and place in the box between the bowls, alternating the direction of the skin sides.
3. Place the Stilton pieces in a line starting at the center and moving to one edge of the box.
4. Fill in any gaps with the almonds and blueberries. Garnish with the mint sprigs.

Let's Play the Harmonica!

If you're spending the night out under the stars, and you happen to have the most popular wind instrument in the world on hand, why not break it out? Here's some music to get you started.

Reading Music:

Harmonica music, called tablature, is easy to read. You don't even have to know how to read standard music notation!

The number denotes which hole on the harmonica to play into. A vertical line above the number denotes blowing out (a blow note):

Example: $\overset{|}{4}$ means to blow out on hole 4.

A vertical line below the number denotes breathing in (a draw note):

Example: $\underset{|}{4}$ means to breathe in on hole 4.

Sometimes you'll see the numbers grouped closer together. This means to play all those notes simultaneously.

Example:

```
|       |      |||
4   4   5   4  345
    |       |
```

Hole 4 is blown out and then drawn in. Next, hole 5 is blown out followed by the draw on hole 4. Finally, holes 3, 4, and 5 are all blown at the same time.

Simple Melodies:

Now you're going to play some songs. Remember, one of your goals here is to be able to produce clean, clear single notes. Observe the space in between the tablatures as a pause, or rest.

Oh Susanna

```
|   | | |   | | |   | |   |
4 4 5 6 6 6 6 5 4 4 5 5 4 4 4
  |       |       |     |   |

|   | | |   | | |   | |     |
4 4 5 6 6 6 6 5 4 4 5 5 4 4 4
  |       |       |     | |

          | | | |
5 5 6 6   6 6 5 4 4
| | | |           |

|   | | |   | | |   | |     |
4 4 5 6 6 6 6 5 4 4 5 5 4 4 4
  |       |       |     | |
```

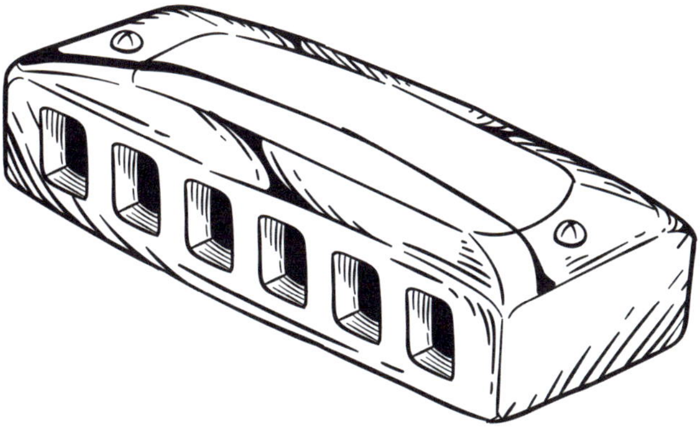

Oh Shenandoah

```
| | | |     | |   |   |       |   | | |
3 4 4 4   4 5 6 6 6   7 7 6   6 6 6 5 6
          |     |       | |     |

        | | |   |   | |   | |   |
6 6 6   5 6 5 4 4   3 4   3 4 6 6
| | |         |               |

| |   |   |   |
3 4 4 5   4 4 4
    |       |
```

When the Saints Go Marching In

```
| |   |   | |   |   | |   | | | |
4 5 5 6   4 5 5 6   4 5 5 6 5 4 5 4
    |         |         |         |

|   | | | | | |     |   | | |   |
5 4 4 4 5 6 6 6 5   5 5 6 5 4 4 4
  |             |     |       |
```

You Are My Sunshine

```
| |   | |   |   | | |   |   |         |   |
3 4 4 5 5   5 4 5 4 4   4 4 5 5 6   6 6 5 5
    |         |           |   | |   |   |

|   |         |   | |   |   |       | |
4 4 5 5 6   6 6 5 5 4   4 4 5 5 4 4 5 4
  |   | |   |   |         |   | | |
```

"A national park is not a playground. It's a sanctuary for nature and for humans who will accept nature on nature's own terms."

Michael Frome, writer, educator, and conservationist

"The parks are the Nation's pleasure grounds and the Nation's restoring places.... The national parks...are an American idea; it is one thing we have that has not been imported."

J. Horace McFarland, president,
American Civic Association, 1916

"Walk away quietly in any direction and taste the freedom of the mountaineer.... Nature's peace will flow into you as sunshine flows into trees. ... As age comes on, one source of enjoyment after another is closed, but nature's sources never fail."

John Muir, naturalist and author known as "Father of the National Parks"

"If future generations are to remember us with gratitude rather than contempt, we must leave them something more than the miracles of technology. We must leave them a glimpse of the world as it was in the beginning, not just after we got through it."

President Lyndon B. Johnson

Spot the 10 Differences!
(answer key)

puzzle on page 110

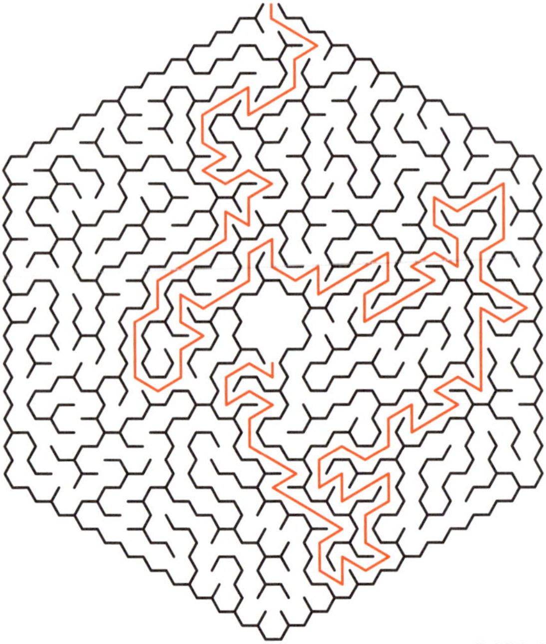

maze on page 8

maze on page 9

maze on page 10

maze on page 11

maze on page 12

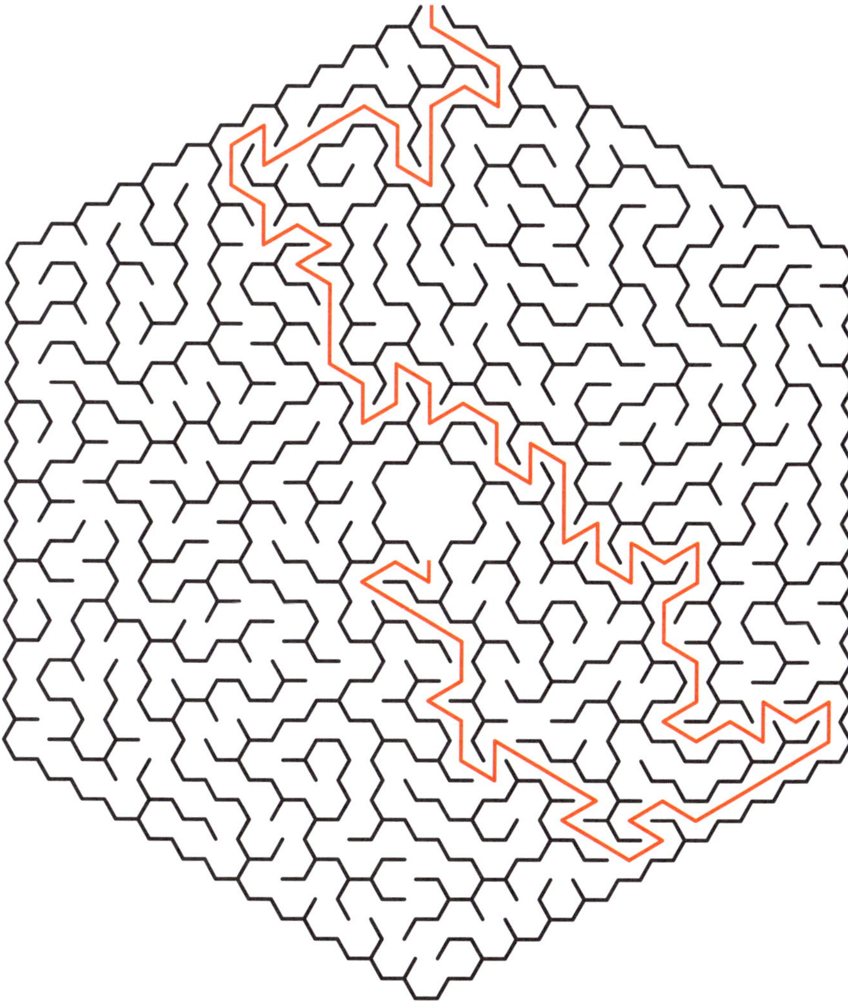

maze on page 13

maze on page 14

maze on page 15

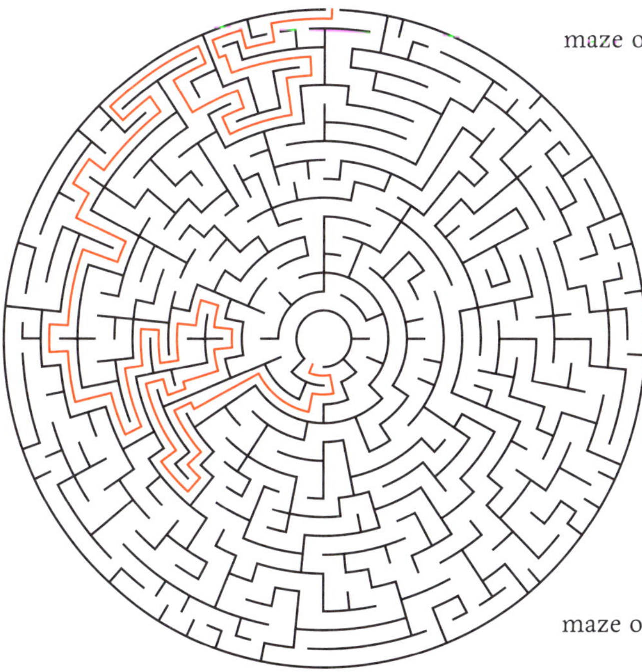

maze on page 16

Test Your Geography!

(answer key)

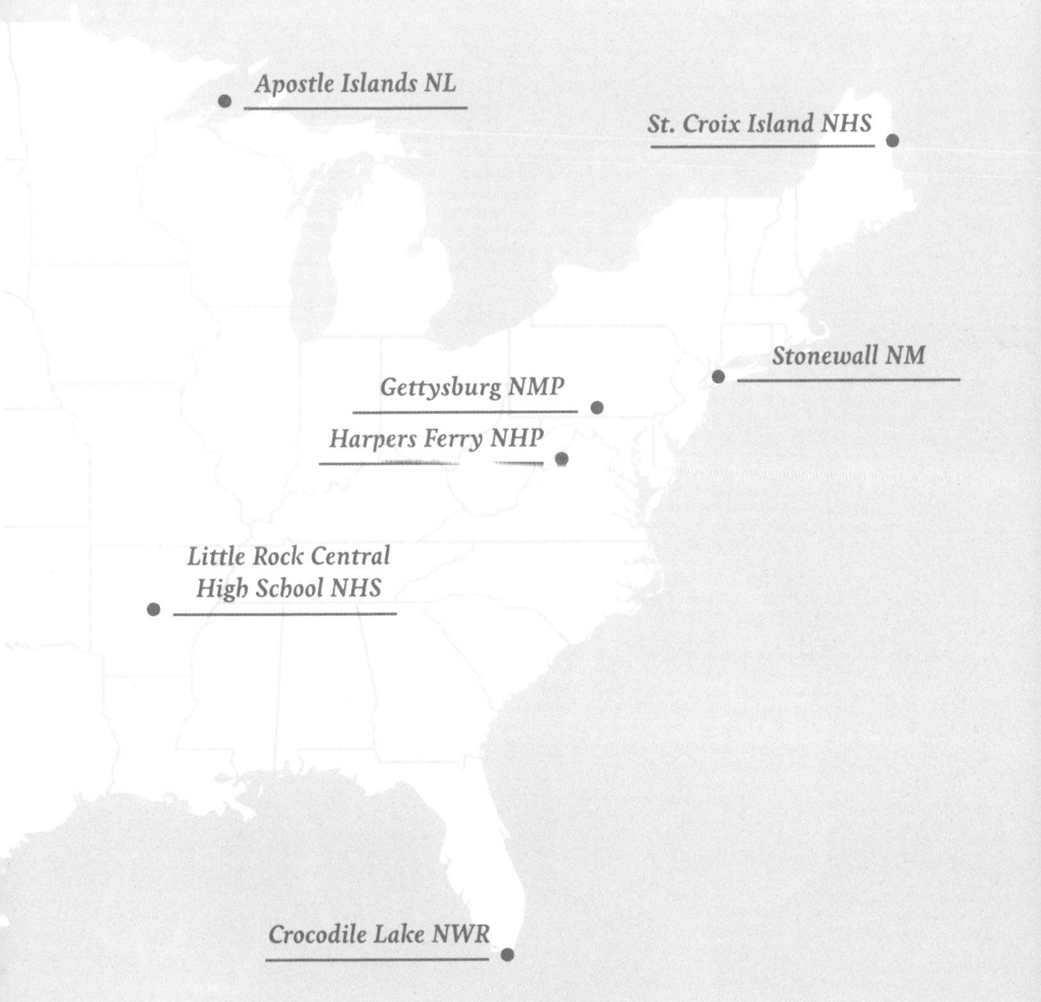

puzzle on page 44

Match the Sticker!

(answer key)

sticker on page 30

sticker on page 18

sticker on page 83

sticker on page 86

sticker on page 31
sticker on page 19
sticker on page 90
sticker on page 27
answers on page 170

Match the Sticker!

(answer key)

sticker on page 154

sticker on page 126

sticker on page 119

sticker on page 179

sticker on page 186

sticker on page 123

sticker on page 114

sticker on page 191

puzzle on page 130

Trivia I

(answer key)

What was the first official National Park, established in 1872?

- ☑ Yosemite
- ○ Yellowstone
- ○ Mount Rushmore
- ○ Grand Canyon

When was the National Park Service established?

- ○ 1871
- ○ 1900
- ○ 1963
- ☑ 1916

Which state has the most official national parks?

- ☑ California
- ○ Alaska
- ○ Utah
- ○ Colorado

How many national parks, monuments, and historic sites are in the United States (as of 2024)?

- ○ 185
- ○ 63
- ☑ 430
- ○ 346

Which national park is situated entirely south of the equator?

- ○ Virgin Islands National Park
- ☑ National Park of American Samoa
- ○ Everglades National Park
- ○ Channel Islands National Park

Which of the following is NOT one of the 19 "designated names" or units in the National Park System?

- ☑ National Mountain Peak
- ○ National Military Park
- ○ National Recreation Area
- ○ National Lakeshore

trivia on page 48

Trivia II

(answer key)

What is skijoring?

- ○ A sport where a person on a sled is pulled by dogs
- ○ A sport where a person cross-country skis, periodically stopping to shoot at a target
- ✓ A sport where a person on skis is pulled by horses, dogs, or a snowmobile
- ○ A sport where a person skis over a frozen lake

Which national park has its own commercial airport?

- ✓ Grand Teton (Wyoming)
- ○ Denali (Alaska)
- ○ Glacier (Montana)
- ○ Arches (Utah)

Which national park can be reached only by boat or aircraft?

- ○ Katmai (Alaska)
- ○ Dry Tortugas (Florida)
- ○ Isle Royale (Michigan)
- ✓ All of the above

As of 2024, which of the following was NOT part of the National Park system?

- ○ Castle Hill Lighthouse (Rhode Island)
- ✓ Historic U.S. Highway 66
- ○ Alcatraz Island (California)
- ○ Brooklyn Bridge (New York)

What is the most visited national monument?

- ○ Muir Woods (California
- ○ Devils Tower (Wyoming)
- ✓ Statue of Liberty (New York)
- ○ Grand Staircase-Escalante (Utah)

Which of the following national parks does NOT have sand dunes?

- ○ Death Valley (California)
- ○ Kobuk Valley (Alaska)
- ○ Indiana Dunes (Indiana)
- ✓ Great Basin (Nevada)

trivia on page 133

Sudoku

(answer key)

8	3	5	9	2	1	4	6	7
1	9	7	4	6	5	2	3	8
4	6	2	3	7	8	1	5	9
3	2	8	5	9	4	6	7	1
7	5	4	6	1	3	9	8	2
9	1	6	7	8	2	5	4	3
2	4	9	8	5	7	3	1	6
5	8	1	2	3	6	7	9	4
6	7	3	1	4	9	8	2	5

puzzle on page 132

5	8	4	9	1	2	6	3	7
9	2	1	6	7	3	4	5	8
6	7	3	5	4	8	9	2	1
2	9	6	1	3	4	7	8	5
3	1	5	7	8	9	2	4	6
8	4	7	2	6	5	1	9	3
7	5	9	8	2	6	3	1	4
1	3	2	4	5	7	8	6	9
4	6	8	3	9	1	5	7	2

puzzle on page 134

"In particularly tough times, we fall back on these questions of who we are, where do we come from. The national parks are our best idea and therefore, are the places where we can find the answers to those questions."

Ken Burns, filmmaker

"Without wilderness, we will eventually lose the capacity to understand America. Our drive, our ruggedness, our unquenchable optimism and zeal and elan go back to the challenges of the untrammeled wilderness."

Harvey Broome, cofounder of The Wilderness Society

"As strenuous challenge or contemplative retreat, the parks and other units of the national lands offer welcome respite from the world, a safety valve for body and spirit."

T. H. Watkins, historian and environmental writer

"But our national heritage
is richer than just scenic
features; the realization is coming
that perhaps our greatest national
heritage is nature itself."

Fauna of the National Parks of the United States